MW00396206

Antonio Carlos **Jobim**
for classical guitar

Arranged by
Paulo **Bellinati**

Online Video

You Tube
www.melbay.com/99725V

Video
dv.melbay.com/99725

1 2 3 4 5 6 7 8 9 0

Visit us on the Web at www.melbay.com — E-mail us at email@melbay.com
Visit Paulo Bellinati on the Web at www.bellinati.com

TABLE OF CONTENTS

FOREWORD

In 1999 I began to select the compositions and conceive the arrangements contained in this book. After recording the *Paulo Bellinati Plays Antonio Carlos Jobim* video (Mel Bay Publications) in 2001, I started the actual work of writing the material in order to produce the most accurate guitar parts for every single piece recorded on the video. For a number of reasons, it took me much longer than I'd planned, and I only managed to wind up the work on the remaining two scores at the beginning of 2006, adding the final fingering and dynamic indications. I'm very proud to finally make this project available to everyone who loves to play this refined repertoire.

One seldom finds printed popular music that contains more than melody and chord symbols. An accurate transcription of a popular work that contains all the events that go on in an instrumental performance is even more rare. My desire to fill in this void, coupled with my deep love of Jobim's music as well as the possibility of having many other guitarists play my arrangements in the future, swayed me into tackling this project.

My main goal was to transpose the universe of this masterful Brazilian composer to the guitar. Jobim was a well-respected arranger who was highly attentive to details; his extreme good taste emerged not only in his sublime melodies and harmonies but also in all the other finishing parameters of a musical work such as introductions, counterpoint, improvisations, dynamics, nuances, and even rhythmic details of the accompaniment. Moreover, I intended to present quite a different Jobim from the one who came up with "Garota de Ipanema" and "One Note Samba"; these and so many others, but by no means less wonderful Bossa Nova standards, were not the pieces I was looking for while assembling this collection.

First of all, I've worked over the songs with real possibilities to be transposed for solo guitar, more precisely, the ones without lyrics, such as "Bate-Boca", "Antigua", "Garoto", "Valsa do Porto das Caixas", and "Surfboard", originally instrumental works that reveal a much more sophisticated Jobim, closer to his favorite classical composers such as Debussy, Ravel, Chopin, Gnattali, and Villa-Lobos.

Secondly, the songs of more introspective and romantic character like "Estrada Branca" (the oldest Jobim piece in this book, first recorded in 1958 by Elizeth Cardoso), "Amparo", "Gabriela", "Por Toda a Minha Vida", "Chora Coração", "A Felicidade" (the famous theme from the motion picture *Black Orpheus*) and "Luiza", the most beautiful and perfect Brazilian song ever written. Unfortunately, "Gabriela" and "Amparo" had to be left out of this collection due to unacceptable contractual demands made by the copyright owners. I hope I will be able to include these missing arrangements in a future printing.

Another goal of this publication was to contribute to the Brazilian solo guitar literature, which has been played and recorded by increasingly more soloists around the world. The musical consistency of the pieces presented here certainly will move artists to include some of them in their concert program, side by side with other masterpieces written by Villa-Lobos, Pernambuco, Garoto, Gnattali, Mignone and other great maestros from Brazil.

My previous publication *The Guitar Works of Garoto* (GSP-1990) - two volumes of folios with the music of the great Brazilian guitarist Annibal Augusto Sardinha (Garoto) was a challenge in the sense that my goal was to recover an original guitar work that had been lost. I even wrote a couple of arrangements, but for most of the pieces, the main body of work was to transcribe note by note from Garoto's original recordings and/or manuscripts.

For this Jobim project I faced an even greater challenge, all the pieces here have been arranged and re-created, completely written out from scratch, based on Jobim's original recordings alone. I did not use any previous guitar version even as a simple reference, except for my own versions of "Luiza" and "Garoto" recorded on my *Serenata* CD (GSP 1993).

Hoping this book fulfills most of the aspirations stated above, I sincerely wish, dear colleague, you will have as much fun reading and playing these pieces as I have had all these years.

Enjoy!

Paulo Bellinati

São Paulo

"This book is dedicated to my family and friends who love Jobim's music as much as I do. They gave me the energy, support and inspiration to complete this project.

I sincerely thank Claudia Simões for the wonderful watercolor she painted especially for the cover, Branko Kukurin for the picture of me taken at the live concert at the 2004 Kastav Guitar Festival-Croacia, Marcílio Godoi for all the graphic ideas and the digital treatment of the cover art, Daniel Murray for first reading all the pieces, searching for (and finding) occasional mistakes in my manuscript, Mirella Zilli Celeri for the English version of the Jobim biography, José Murray for asking me to include "Bate-Boca" in the repertoire, Claudio Leal Ferreira for the lead sheet of "Valsa do Porto das Caixas", Cristina Azuma for having flown from Paris to the U.S. especially to play "Amparo" with me on the video, Edgard Poças for the excellent suggestions during my research, Rick Udler and Jerry Udler for the English proof-reading/editing of the texts in this book, and Bill Bay for making this project come true.

A special thanks to my friends Alan and Esther Haddad for their generous help and constant encouragement ever since this project was first conceived.

I'm also very grateful to my dear friends and excellent musicians Carlos Barbosa-Lima, Sergio Sarraceni, and Luiz Roberto Oliveira, for providing me with the honor to meet Jobim personally, and for always believing in my work.

Finally, I want to thank my dear wife, Fernanda de Castro, from the bottom of my heart, and my wonderful kids, Carlo and Giulia, for their endless love and for making my life complete.

Paulo Bellinati

Antonio Carlos Brasileiro de Almeida Jobim was born on January 25th, 1927 in Rio de Janeiro, and lived most of his youth in the Ipanema neighborhood. His first instrument was the guitar and then he took up the piano. Initial classes with the renowned Hans Joachim Koellreuter were followed by further piano studies under Lucia Branco and Thomás Teran, and orchestral arranging under Leo Peracchi. As an architecture undergraduate Jobim did a brief stint at an architecture office. Upon realizing his true calling he abandoned all other vocational pursuits in order to become a professional pianist and to study harmony.

In 1949 he married his high-school sweetheart, Tereza, making ends meet by playing at Rio de Janeiro nightclubs. Three years later, he was hired by Continental Records where he wrote arrangements for important singers such as Dalva de Oliveira, Orlando Silva, Elizeth Cardoso, and Dick Farney. At that time the main arranger at Continental was Radamés Gnattali, who coached Jobim as his musical godson.

In 1953 "Incerteza", co-authored with Newton Mendonça, was his first song to be recorded. In 1954, singers Dick Farney and Lúcio Alves did a duet recording of "Tereza da Praia", co-authored with Billy Blanco which became his first hit. He and Billy Blanco also composed the music for the album *Sinfonia do Rio de Janeiro*, with arrangements by Radamés Gnattali, which was later included in the soundtrack of *Esse Rio Que Eu Amo*, a Hugo Christensen film. Amongst the first singers to record his music were Nora Ney and Elizeth Cardoso who attracted serious attention to the talent of this young composer.

In 1956 Jobim met the legendary poet and lyricist Vinicius de Moraes, who invited him that very year, to compose the music for his play *Orfeu da Conceição,* which was presented at the Municipal Theatre of Rio de Janeiro, the album being released on EMI subsidiary Odeon. The Jobim-penned samba "A Felicidade" (lyrics by Vinicius de Moraes) was included in the Marcel Camus film *Black Orpheus*, which received the 1959 Palm d'Or at the Cannes Film Festival, and the Oscar for Best Foreign Film in 1960.

The Sylvia Telles album, *Carícia*, released in 1956, included the hit "Foi a Noite", co-authored with Newton Mendonça. The groundbreaking "Chega de Saudade", composed with Vinicius de Moraes, was a major hallmark in his career and in the history of Brazilian music. Released in 1958 on the Elizeth Cardoso album "Canção do Amor Demais", with musical direction and orchestral arrangements by the composer, introduced João Gilberto's innovative guitar accompaniment.

In 1959, João Gilberto's first album, "Chega de Saudade" (Odeon), featured the title song as well as "Desafinado" (Jobim-Mendonça), two breathtaking sambas which launched the Bossa Nova movement thereby radically changing the face of Brazilian popular music forever. That same year six of his songs including "Desafinado" became big hits, three of them co-authored with Vinicius de Moraes; "Eu Sei Que Vou Te Amar", "A Felicidade", "Brigas Nunca Mais", plus "Dindi", with Aloysio de Oliveira, and "Este Seu Olhar".

In 1962 Jobim and Vinicius de Moraes composed "Garota de Ipanema", one of the most widely recorded songs in the world. On November 21 of that same year, he performed with other artists at the legendary Bossa Nova show at Carnegie Hall in New York. He composed the soundtrack for Paulo César Sarraceni´s film *Porto das Caixas* that year as well.

Between 1963 and 1964 he recorded two albums in the United States: *The Composer of Desafinado Plays* (Verve) and *The Wonderful World of Antonio Carlos Jobim* (Warner), which included "Por Toda a Minha Vida", "Valsa do Porto das Caixas" and "Surfboard". During this period Jobim established Corcovado Music, his own publishing company, in the USA. He also made a guest appearance on the Sérgio Mendes-led *Bossa Nova York* album featuring Art Farmer among others.

First-rate jazz musicians such as Ella Fitzgerald, Coleman Hawkins, Curtis Fuller, Zoot Sims, Herbie Mann and Dizzy Gillespie started recording his music. The *Getz/Gilberto* (Verve) album, featuring Antonio Carlos Jobim, sold two million copies the first year alone.

In 1964 in Brazil, he recorded the classic album *Caymmi Visita Tom* (Elenco) with Dorival Caymmi and family. When they got together to record the album, Caymmi's gift to Jobim was a samba-cum-waltz number, "Das Rosas," to which Jobim responded with another new song "Só Tinha de Ser Com Você". That same year he also composed the soundtrack for Sacha Gordine´s film *Santo Módico*.

In 1965 Jobim recorded the album *A Certain Mr. Jobim* (Warner) with arrangements by Claus Ogerman. Two years later, he recorded the album *Francis Albert Sinatra & Antônio Carlos Jobim* (Reprise) which won the Grammy Award for best Vocal aAbum of the year. Jobim's success in the United States was extraordinary, second only to The Beatles in sales.

Riding on the wave of music festivals, which exploded in Brazil during the 1960s, "Sabiá", co-authored with Chico Buarque, was performed at the 3rd International Song Festival in 1968, winning first prize and receiving one of the longest ovations in the history of Brazilian music festivals.

Between 1967 and 1970 further U.S. releases followed: *Wave* (A&M), whose title track has become a standard, *Tide* (A&M) - both arranged by Claus Ogerman, and *Stone Flower* (CTI), with arrangements by Eumir Deodato, including instrumental hits "Amparo" and "Garoto". In 1970 he composed the soundtrack for the Louis Gilbert film *The Adventurers*. The second sessions with Frank Sinatra, produced by Eumir Deodato, took place in 1969 with the tracks being issued in 1971 under the title, *Sinatra and Company* (Reprise).

The album *Matita Perê* (MCA/Philips) released in 1973 included the classic "Águas de Março" as well as "Crônica da Casa Assassinada" - a four-piece suite that became the soundtrack to another Paulo César Saraceni film. Another version of "Águas de Março," which Jobim recorded with Elis Regina in 1974 on the album *Elis & Tom* (Philips/Verve), went on to become one of his most successful hits. In 1977 Jobim recorded the album *Miucha & Antônio Carlos Jobim* (RCA), as well as the live album *Tom, Vinicius, Toquinho & Miucha* in Rio de Janeiro at the Canecão.

Jobim composed the music for several movies: *Eu Te Amo* (1980) a film by Arnaldo Jabor, *Gabriela* (1982) by Bruno Barreto, and *Para Viver Um Grande Amor* (1983) by Miguel Faria Júnior, which was also released as an album on Columbia.

In the late 1970s/early 1980s, important albums such as *Urubu* (1975-Warner), *Terra Brasilis* (1980-Warner), *Edu e Tom* (1981-Philips), *Tom Jobim e Billy Blanco* (1983-Relevo) the soundtrack, *Gabriela* (1983-BMG), and *O Tempo e o Vento* (1985-Som Livre) were released. In 1984, he formed the group Banda Nova, which performed at Carnegie Hall. The following year, he performed with João Gilberto at the Montreux Festival, Switzerland. In 1987, he and his Banda Nova recorded the albums *Tom Jobim Inédito* (BMG) and *Passarim* (Verve), which included the hit "Luiza", composed for the TV soap opera *Brilhante* (TV Globo).

In 1990 Jobim recorded another live album *Tom canta Vinicius* which was finally released by Jobim Music in ten years later.

In 1992, at Rio de Janeiro's carnival parade, 'Estação Primeira de Mangueira' samba school paid tribute to Jobim's life and music with the theme "Se Todos Fossem Iguais A Você", the same title as the song that he composed with Vinicius de Moraes in the 1950s. In 1994 he released *Antônio Brasileiro*; the album won a Grammy in the Best Latin Jazz Performance category.

Antonio Carlos Jobim passed away on December 8th, 1994 following post-surgical complications at Mount Sinai Medical Center in New York City. He had traveled to the U.S. for bladder cancer treatment. His songs have been recorded and performed by artists throughout the world, and his legacy to the Brazilian music repertoire is an incalculable treasure.

PAULO BELLINATI

Born in São Paulo in 1950, Paulo Bellinati is one of Brazil's most accomplished contemporary guitarists. He studied classical guitar with Isaias Sávio and graduated from the Conservatory Dramático e Musical of São Paulo. From 1975 to 1980, Bellinati lived in Switzerland, continuing his musical studies at the Conservatory of Geneva and teaching at the Conservatory of Lausanne. At that time he also performed with his own group in many European festivals including the Montreux Jazz Festival, the Ozone Jazz Festival in Neuchâtel, and the Festival du Bois de La Batîe in Geneva.

Besides performing solo concerts and giving master classes in many international guitar festivals, he also tours with different ensembles including his own guitar trio, the Pau Brasil group, and with the Brazilian singer Mônica Salmaso. He has both recorded and performed with these and other important artists including Steve Swallow, Carla Bley, Gal Costa, Renaud Garcia-Fons, Antonio Placer, Leila Pinheiro, João Bosco, Cesar Camargo Mariano, Edu Lobo and Chico Buarque.

Aside from being a performer, composer and arranger, Bellinati is also a respected musical scholar. He rediscovered, transcribed and recorded the music of the great Brazilian guitarist-composer Annibal Augusto Sardinha (Garoto). His landmark recording *The Guitar Works of Garoto* (GSP) and two-volume edition of Garoto's works have received international critical acclaim and recognition for their historical significance.

Paulo Bellinati draws from the rich tradition of Brazil, and most of his compositions are written in Brazilian musical styles such as: Lundu, Modinha, Schottisch, Choro, Seresta, Maxixe, Jongo, Samba, Valsa Serenata, Baião, Maracatu, Frevo, and Xaxado. He has developed a contemporary approach to Brazilian folklore, enhancing traditional forms with modern compositional techniques and harmonies.

He has written arrangements for guitar solo, duo and trio, guitar & clarinet, guitar & voice, and for many different ensembles. Some of these works have been recorded on his albums *New Choros of Brazil* (Acoustic Music Records), *A Felicidade* (GSP), and *Afro-Sambas* (GSP), with vocalist Mônica Salmaso featuring Paulo's arrangements of the complete afro-sambas by composers Baden Powell and Vinicius de Moraes.

He has won numerous awards, including the *Guitar Player* magazine poll as one of the top 10 Brazilian guitarists, the 1994 Prêmio Sharp awards (Brazilian Grammy) as best arranger for Gal Costa's CD *O Sorriso do Gato de Alice*. He also received the Prêmio Sharp nomination as best soloist for his albums *Serenata* (GSP), and *Lira Brasileira* (GSP). His *Garoto* album received a 5-star rating from *CD Review*, and the album *Guitares du Brésil* (GHA) received "Le Choc de La Musique", the highest award from the prestigious Le Monde de la Musique in France.

In 1988, Paulo Bellinati won the first prize in composition for his solo guitar piece "Jongo", at the 8th Carrefour Mondial de la Guitare in Martinique. In 1996, John Williams & Timothy Kain recorded "Jongo" (guitar duet version) for their album *The Mantis and the Moon*.

In 1998 Paulo Bellinati recorded the *Brazilian Guitar Virtuoso* DVD for Mel Bay Publications, performing and discussing his compositions. In 2003 Mel Bay released the *Paulo Bellinati Plays Antonio Carlos Jobim* DVD, which includes Paulo's arrangements of some of the masterpieces by the great Brazilian composer Antonio Carlos Jobim.

His most important recent projects include this volume of folios *Antonio Carlos Jobim for Classical Guitar*, the publication of his piece "Lun-Duo" (GSP) for two guitars, the release of his solo album *A Felicidade* (GSP-2008), the Pau Brasil group recording *2005* (Biscoito Fino), and the Mônica Salmaso/Pau Brasil recording *Noites de Gala, Samba Na Rua* (Biscoito Fino-2007).

Fingerprint barré

Played with the 1st joint of the finger indicated on the score.
In most cases the 1st joint is relaxed and allows the fingertip to
bend backwards (as if to bend backward as though leaving the
fingerprint on the fingerboard).
In the example, the hand position allows the simultaneous playing
of two bass notes (E and B) with the *fingerprint barré* and higher notes
(F# and A) with fingers 4 and 2.

Estrada Branca

Crossing barré

The 1st finger, in a curved position, presses a note on a bass string
and a note on the first or second string a fret lower simultaneously.
In the example the 1st finger plays an A with the 3rd joint (the one
closest to the palm) and a D-sharp with the fingertip.

Bate-Boca

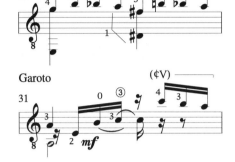

Barré in parenthesis (a)

Used for better mechanical solutions.
In the example, a half-barré on the 5th fret presses the 4
treble strings, and allows a precise move to the next measure.

Garoto

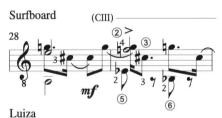

Barré in parenthesis (b)

Allows the left-hand fingers the maximum stretch.
In the example, the 1st finger plays the 1st string using the 3rd
joint only. The finger stays straight as in a full barré position
but the fingertip is pointing away from the fingerboard.

Surfboard

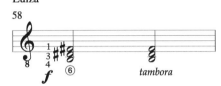

Tambora

tambora

A traditional percussive effect produced by hitting the side of
the right-hand thumb against the strings close to the bridge.
In the example, the B Major chord should ring clearly by
striking only the bass strings.

Luiza

Left hand only / right hand only

l.h.   r.h.

l.h. Hammer-on the note using only the left-hand finger.
r.h. Tap the note using only the right-hand finger.
In the example the notes are played on the 2nd string;
finger 4 hammers on the C sharp and the right-hand index
finger taps the D sharp.

Luiza

Natural and artificial harmonics

har.
XII
◇

The diamond-shaped noteheads (harmonics) are at actual pitch (concert).
Normal noteheads sound an octave lower than written.
The example is a combination of harmonics and normal sounds.
The first beat is a chord with the A bass string and two natural harmonics
(E on the 1st string-12th fret and D on the 3rd string-7th fret) followed by
a melody in artificial harmonics.

Chora Coração

Glissando slur

Indicated by a line over/under the noteheads.
The finger number appears only on the first note and the
second note is not plucked by the right hand.
The example shows a descending *glissando slur* with the 1st finger.

A Felicidade

Glissando of expression

Indicated by a line between the affected notes with finger numbers
on both. Occurs naturally in a change of position.
The second note must be plucked by the right hand as well.
The example shows two chords connected by a *glissando of expression*.

A Felicidade

Estrada Branca

Arranged by
Paulo Bellinati

for solo guitar

Antonio Carlos Jobim
(1927-1994)

12

※ The artificial C sharp harmonic is played while the first finger of the left hand presses the F sharp on the second fret of the first string.

Bate-Boca

Arranged by
Paulo Bellinati

for solo guitar

Antonio Carlos Jobim
(1927-1994)

16

❋ The top C is also played pizzicato with the thumb. Finger 4 presses the 1st string over the (imaginary) 20th fret location.

Luiza

Arranged by
Paulo Bellinati

for solo guitar

Antonio Carlos Jobim
(1927-1994)

※   In some recordings, Jobim plays a G natural one half-step higher than the written F sharp.

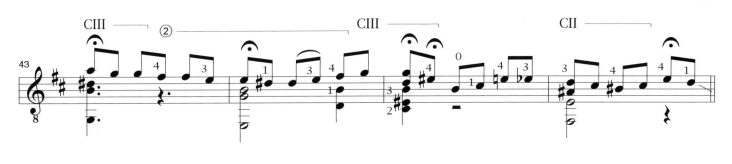

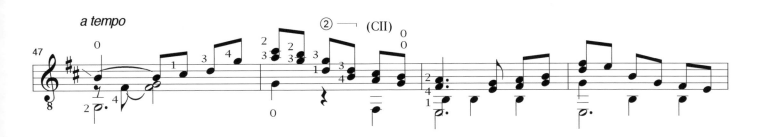

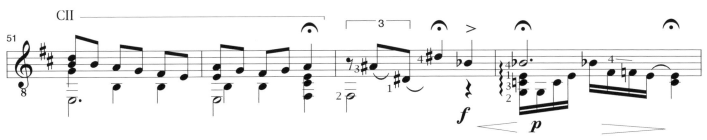

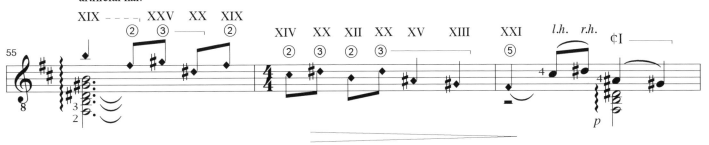

Por Toda a Minha Vida

Arranged by
Paulo Bellinati

for solo guitar

Antonio Carlos Jobim
(1927-1994)

Antigua

Arranged by
Paulo Bellinati

for solo guitar

Antonio Carlos Jobim
(1927-1994)

♩ = 70   Tempo de Bossa

Chora Coração

Arranged by
Paulo Bellinati

for solo guitar

Antonio Carlos Jobim
(1927-1994)

28

Garoto
(Choro)

for solo guitar

Arranged by
Paulo Bellinati

Antonio Carlos Jobim
(1927-1994)

Valsa do Porto das Caixas

Arranged by
Paulo Bellinati

for solo guitar

Antonio Carlos Jobim
(1927-1994)

※ The artificial A and D harmonics are played while the left-hand first finger (barré) presses the D (2nd string) and the G (1st string).

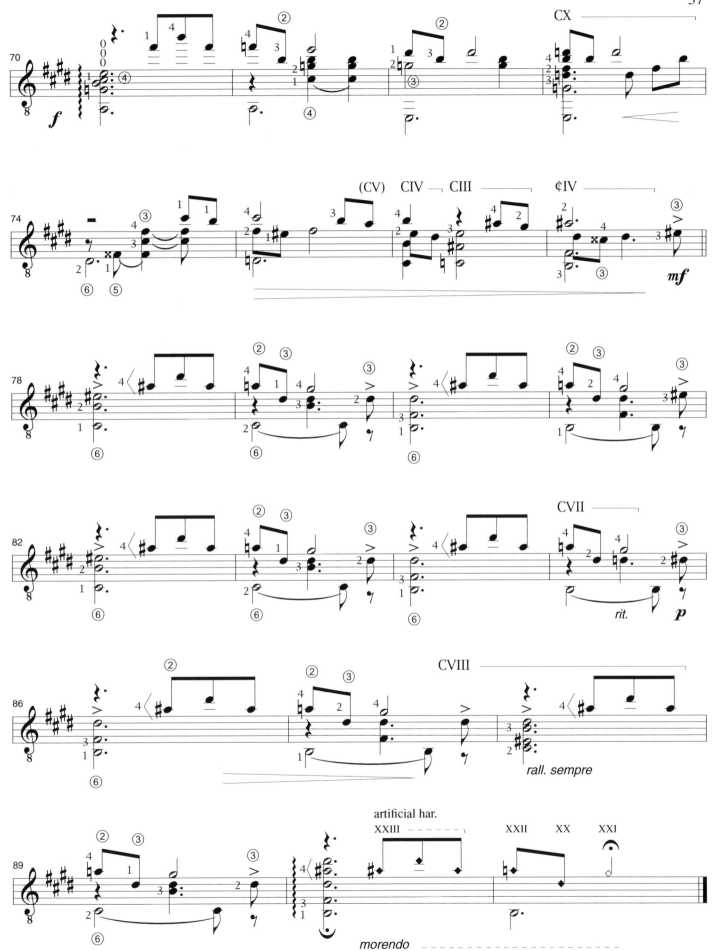

A Felicidade

Arranged by
Paulo Bellinati

for solo guitar

Antonio Carlos Jobim
(1927-1994)

40

Improvisando

Surfboard

Arranged by
Paulo Bellinati

for solo guitar

Antonio Carlos Jobim
(1927-1994)

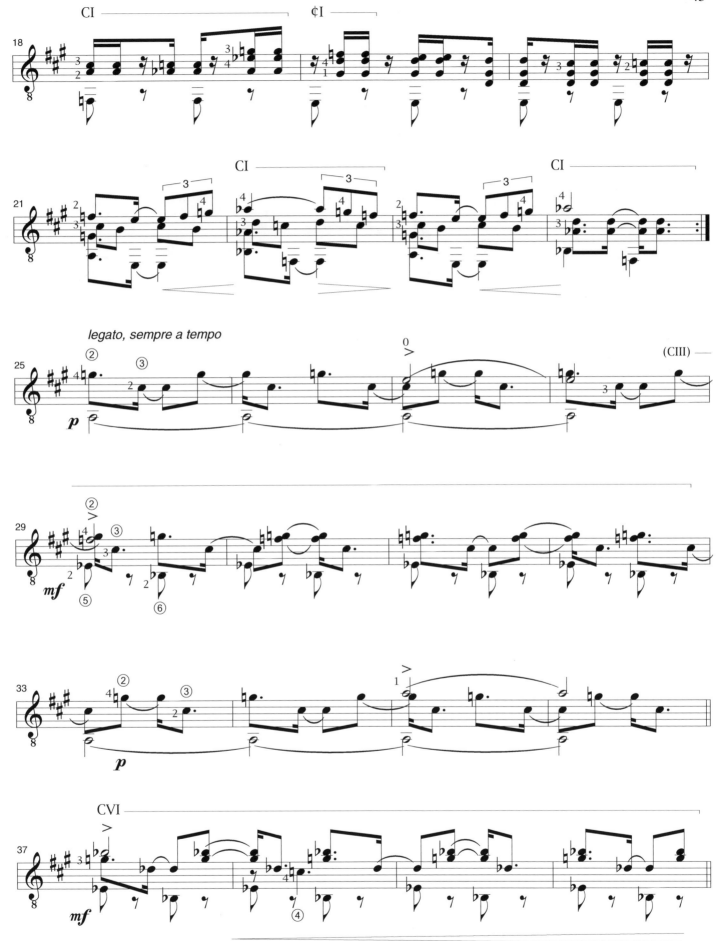

sempre preciso

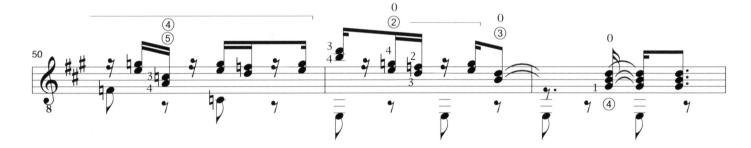

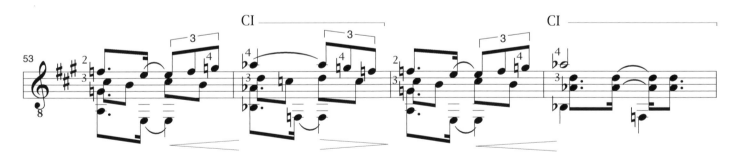

Simile prima